W9-DIY-187

Machines at Work

Helicopters

by Cari Meister

Bullfrog Books

Ideas for Parents and Teachers

Bullfrog Books let children practice nonfiction reading at the earliest reading levels. Repetition, familiar words, and photo labels support early readers.

Before Reading

- Discuss the cover photo. What does it tell them?

- Look at the picture glossary together. Read and discuss the words.

Read the Book

- "Walk" through the book and look at the photos. Let the child ask questions. Point out the photo labels.

- Read the book to the child, or have him or her read independently.

After Reading

- Prompt the child to think more. Ask: What other things do you think a helicopter can do? Where have you seen a helicopter? What was it doing?

Bullfrog Books are published by Jump!
5357 Penn Avenue South
Minneapolis, MN 55419
www.jumplibrary.com

Library of Congress Cataloging-in-Publication Data
Meister, Cari.
  Helicopters / by Cari Meister.
    pages cm -- (Bullfrog books. Machines at work)
  Includes bibliographical references and index.
  Summary: "This photo-illustrated book for early readers tells about the parts of a helicopter, how it works, and how people use helicopters for transportation and rescue"-- Provided by publisher.
  Audience: Grades K to grade 3.
  ISBN 978-1-62031-046-5 (hardcover : alk. paper) -- ISBN 978-1-62496-058-1 (ebook)
  1. Helicopters--Juvenile literature. I. Title.
  TL716.2.M45 2014
  629.133'352--dc23
                                        2012042018

Series Editor: Rebecca Glaser
Book Editor: Patrick Perish
Series Designer: Ellen Huber
Book Designer: Sara Pokorny

Photo Credits:
123RF, 5, 23bl, 24; Alamy, 16, 17; Dreamstime, cover, 4, 14; Shutterstock, 1, 3, 6, 8, 11, 12, 15, 18, 19, 21, 22, 23tl, 23br; SuperStock, 7, 13, 23tr

Printed in the United States of America at Corporate Graphics in North Mankato, Minnesota.
5-2013 / PO 1003
10 9 8 7 6 5 4 3 2 1

Table of Contents

Helicopters at Work

Whup! Whup! Whup!

Look up.

A helicopter flies in the air.

How does it work?

Look at the rotor blades.

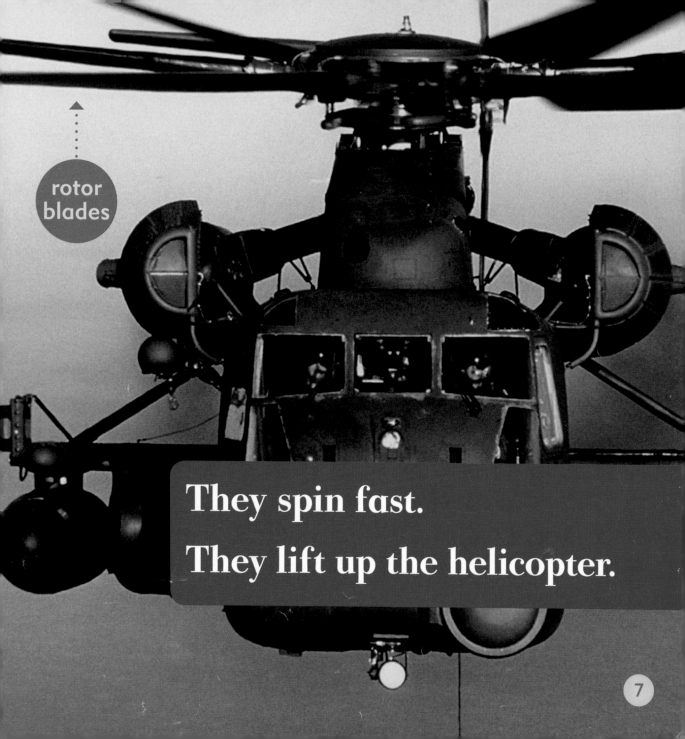

rotor
blades

They spin fast.
They lift up the helicopter.

Look at the tail fin.

tail
fin

It keeps the helicopter steady.

Look at the
landing skids.

The helicopter
lands on them.

landing

control
stick

The pilot sits in the cockpit.
He uses a control stick
to turn.

13

Oh no! A fire!

A helicopter
scoops up water.

The pilot flies low.
He dumps the water.
The fire is out!

Oh no!
A river flooded.
People are stuck.
What can help?
A helicopter!

Oh no!

A man is hurt.

He needs help.

He is put on a stretcher.

Quick! To the hospital!

stretcher

19

Helicopters can do many things!

Parts of a Helicopter

rotor blades
Long, flat pieces that spin and lift the helicopter into the air.

cockpit
The place where the pilot sits.

tail fin
A small piece that helps balance the helicopter.

landing skids
Metal runners that the helicopter lands on.

Picture Glossary

control stick
A lever where the pilot controls the helicopter.

pilot
The person that flies an aircraft, like a helicopter or airplane.

hover
To hang in the air in one place.

stretcher
A carrying device used to move sick or hurt people.

Index

To Learn More

Learning more is as easy as 1, 2, 3.

1) Go to www.factsurfer.com

2) Enter "helicopter" into the search box.

3) Click the "Surf" button to see a list of websites.

With factsurfer.com, finding more information is just a click away.